The Sea at Truro

The Sea at Truro

POEMS

Nancy Willard

Alfred A. Knopf · New York · 2012

THIS IS A BORZOI BOOK
PUBLISHED BY ALFRED A. KNOPF

www.aaknopf.com

Page 79 constitutes an extension of this page.

Library of Congress Cataloging-in-Publication Data
Willard, Nancy.
The sea at Truro : poems / by Nancy Willard.—1st ed.
p.   cm.
"This Is a Borzoi Book."
ISBN 978-0-307-95977-5
I. Title.
PS3573.I444S43 2012
811'.54—dc23
2012008015

Jacket photograph by Eric Lindbloom
Jacket design by Linda Huang

Manufactured in the United States of America
First Edition

For Eric and James

True mysteries are hidden in the light.

—Jean Giono

Contents

I

Calling the Characters

Is this the right house? Shabbier than last time
but when was that? Two weeks ago? Two months?
Have they forgotten me? The door's unlocked,
left open for me or somebody else
who fawns over them, a con man after their money
(do they have any?), who listens to their stories
(have I forgotten them?) over and over again.
How still the house sounds.

They sit on the screened-in porch,
silent as after hearing bad news
or an embarrassing remark. They pay me
no mind. Is it supper already?
When I follow them inside, when I sit
at the one place left for a stranger,
nobody looks at me. Nobody passes me
the plate of cold cuts.

They have not spoken for weeks
but they know I am here.
And now, in voices dipped from a pool
of still water, they say inane things,
talking away at each other, small talk,
though not small, I think, as I listen
to what's left unsaid, as I let myself
into their lives again, as I turn transparent

The third night she stands at the foot of his bed
pleading. She begs him to take the paintings.
Maybe he will have better luck.
Her death? They don't speak of it.
She says, "Take the days as they come,
the nights as they go. Don't forget me."
He says, "How much of yourself you left behind!"
She says, "Look for me in the world I left
when the sun splashes its light on everything."

Bridget's Confession

The two of us running up Fifth Avenue,
Michael, a long leap of a lad
in his black church clothes
and his brother's brogues,
and his hair flying,

and me with my brimmed hat hooping
down the steps of St. Pat's
'til it's cocked on the wind's head,
bent on blowing me clean
out of my senses.

Oh, why did I let that boy go?
God himself loved the sight of us.
I would be the blue light in his eye,
the left one, the farseeing one,
the one he's rubbing now, maybe.

The Famous Poet

At midnight I saw, in our empty street
in Poughkeepsie, the stretch limo
sent by the prelates of poetry to carry
the poet to his distant home.
I am sure that a man whose poems honor
things that do not run on time,
dogs, poems, the weather in Poughkeepsie
did not ask for a limo.
He spoke his poems. To five hundred people

who came to listen, his voice said
"I am speaking these words for you alone,
you who understand the misunderstood dog,
the silence that separates salt and pepper."
Straight as a candle he stood,
his light not a hard gemlike flame
but a pilot light putting us at ease.
We sat in front of his words
and warmed ourselves.

He thanked us, he said goodbye,
and those who invited him
urged him outside to a quieter space,
and fed him and wined him
at the long table of distinguished guests
and sent him home in the dark corridor
of a stretch limousine, which I saw,
and opened our front door to see it better
as it whispered past me into the dark.

Daily News

He lay curled in his mother's pumpkin belly
when a bullet entered his thigh.
The bullet was innocent,
the thigh thinner than a noodle.
They stuck together and made
the best of it.

His mother, sitting on the porch rocking,
never saw who shot her, or the starling
behind her, or the squirrel over her head.
Heard no cry from within,
felt the sleeper twitch,
and settle down.

And he was born with the sign of his times
upon him, a scar almost invisible,
gift of one who never saw what he hit,
a soldier who slept through the action
and who, to this day,
does not know who hurt him.

Oral History 1941

"Ten years into her life, she asked for a bicycle.
The day of her birthday our mother paid cash
for a girl's Schwinn, blue as her parakeet
and bright as a planet seeking a new moon
in the department store that sold everything,
and as my sister wheeled it toward the door
the manager barred her way. 'I'm sorry.
We just got the news: no more bicycles
till after the war.'

Ration stamps, blue and red tickets for sugar,
butter and shoes, Papa away *for the duration*,

my bed not slept in, me curled up on the floor—
if bayonets shattered my bedroom wall
they'd never skewer me, marshmallow child,
camouflaged by blankets. My sister asked
for a hammock. Hammocks were not rationed.
Our mother bought the basic model,
a string shawl

you might hang in the hold of a ship
so slow you'd think yourself motionless
as the equator, rocking from sleep to death,
from death to sleep and back, or in Manila
among the coconut palms. I thought of first grade
and Sylvia Chang and her fleecy coat, blue
as a clear sky and her mother who never spoke
in the dark rented rooms they lived in, and the thin
leaves of the books she read,

paging from back to front, the words
on each page like tracks left by shadows.
'They tied my father's legs to horses. One horse
ran this way, one ran that way. They played
the National Anthem. He wore his uniform.'
'Did your mom tell you that?' 'No. They made
us watch.' I thought of GIs, the dead washed up
on beaches. Each night our mother's heel flattened
the cans we saved

to make—what? Bullets? Guns? Six years into my life,
when my turn came to wish, I called for Kool-Aid,
which I'd never tasted. When Mother slit the paper
    pouch,
the water bled sunsets, and shaved rubies braided their
    way
to the bottom like a crazed hourglass wanting to kill time.
My mother surrendered the sugar, a month's rations
spreading in ghostly plumes, heavy and peaceful
like sleepers dead to the world, losing themselves
in the slow sweet water."

Some Things Should Never
Be Written Down

Some things should never be written down.
The lovesick hummingbird's whistling for love;

the tide of sleep humming toward me
and baited with whispers, *what he said*,
what she said, and my glad heart
packing its dreams for the trip to morning;

the ring of my mother's name
when my grandfather called to her three days
after he died, and she with her arms full
of wind-washed laundry

just freed from the line.

An Angel Considers the Naming of Meat

Whatever this was, with its arms and skirt,
crowned and winged and all-seeing,
it was no mere grazer. *Crown roast,*
butterfly chop, arm pot roast, skirt steak,
eye round. And what's left
is large and curious as a fallen tree,
split open, a breached tomb of roseate marble.
Seven ribs stand up in a sea of fat.
Like rowers they lean into the wind.
Once they rocked as one, in out, in out,
pushed by the breath of the living beast.
Now there is stillness
on the butcher's board, faintly hollowed
by the flesh of animals fallen under the knife
year after year. How can he bear it?

On his fluted rack hang hooks, poles,
a scraper for scrubbing the rough nap
off flesh ripped by the blade,
and a cleaver nipped from a halo of steel.
The electric slicer buzzes and whines,
but the plucked pullets sleep, curled up
in their chilly incubator,
their wings hugging their sides,
dreamless, having lost their heads.
If they had thumbs, they would be sucking them.
Famished, foolish, I am overcome with grief.
The butcher unhooks a sausage, cuts it,
hands me a wafer studded with precious meats.

"You're my first customer. This one's on me."

Tall Man in a Small Place

When I call you for supper
you do not look up.
Alone in the garden
you are not of this world.
Always a good teacher,
you are taking roll.
You encourage the peppers to swell.
You curl the parsley

and poke the onions for pearls.
Your kind of garden: a kinder garden,
an open classroom.
The slow-witted sunflower droops
its head on your hand.
Pay attention to me, it murmurs.
I have grown a new leaf.

Even the priestly corn
nods in your wake.
Or are you the pupil and they
your examiners?
Or do the highest teachers grow
invisible,
as yeast to the baker?
And we are the hands,
not the seed,
not the maker.

Learning by Heart

The teacher who made us learn a poem
each week by the poet of our choice
also told us Cicero's secret
for perfect memory. Invent a house,
and furnish it. Let the settee
be clothes in a line of your poem.

Let the clocks keep its time.
Let the chairs speak as one,
a collective noun, poetry.

Now walk through the house
of its only guest, the poem
on which you may spy
like a new mother, rising at night
to check on her smallest sleeper.
You are also walking
through the body of the poem,
reading its vital signs.
If the poem could be speechless,

it would stand amazed, seeing
itself everywhere unraveled
yet appraising itself,
marveling at this love
unlooked for, this care
for its breaks

and its breath, this faith
in the right word
and its unseen reader.

Lovely Rosa, Crazy Rosa

Lovely Rosa, Crazy Rosa,
Lotus Rosa, rooted in the gardens of Hawaii
on an island which must be beautiful
if it made you,
do not make this trip
through the snows of my country
into the city, into its violent dark.

You have gathered your teacups,
your porcelain locket,
your nicest things.
You will enter the train
like a dead princess bearing her pleasures away.
Rings sag your pockets,
amulets weight you.

"Are you walking into the sea
with four dollars in your purse?
The regular fare is ten."
"Never mind," you say.
"I know the conductors.
Do you understand I am not coming back?
The girl you know died years ago

and her light is still traveling.
Can you take me to the station?
I do not weigh much.
I am bright as a bag of fruit,
and today I composed a dance.
The studio was full of mirrors.
There was nobody in them but me.

I am about to become a star.
Can you hear my heart
counting its small petals?
Love me.
Love me.
Love me."

An Easy Chair

"When they said I would die, even my chair fainted.
My mother turned away,
my friends fled,

not at my knowing but my knowing when.
If I had time I would make my living
support my dying.

I would make this chair
a comfort to flesh
and a throne for shadows."

Auction Block

This steel box—who has the heart to open it?
Nobody? We will open it slowly.
What am I offered for this black flag?
And for this tattoo on a muscular arm torn free—
a Maltese cross inscribed near the shoulder
and a black banner stamped "In Memory of the
Brothers"
and four elastic bands, to keep the words
affixed to the coffin, what am I offered?
And for this jawbone, planted with teeth,
and for this finger, the print on its pad intact,
and for these candles, minted from footsteps

and prayers in procession, what am I offered?
And for this comb that remembers its owner,
clouded with hair and dust starting its long journey
through the galaxy to our first home in the stars,
and for the last words of the dead
and for the waves that carried them through air
poisoned with grief, into the ears of the living,
what am I offered? What am I offered for their absence
from the expensive real estate of your hearts?
What is it worth? In what currency will you pay
for the hard evidence of these lives, these papers,

these lists and letters that escaped the fire,
and for a man's left shoe found in the street,
and one cell from a hair that carries his name in code,
and for the roofless space in the corridors
plucked clean of lives, the light streaming through,
and this room, with no lock and no door,
What will you give me for this lot?
Going once, going twice, are you all done?
I'll throw in the key to the room for nothing.
Friends, tell me: who has the heart to open it?

II

Shoes

Put your best foot forward
and carry no map.
We know the road,
its sorrows, its intentions,
and the places it changed its mind,
stamped with our heel.
We are the armor of footsteps

and the teacher of toes.
We march them in line—
Left right! Left right!
Pressed to the pavement,
we love the gossip of ants.
Stones click their teeth
when we pass.

To the barnacle we are a boat.
To the mouse a shelter.
To the chipmunk a cradle.
Shape-shifters seek us,
knee-high or toeless
or hammered from iron
or cobbled from glass.

Click your heels together.
We will carry you
over the deadly desert.
We are the sisters you never had.
Like you, we wear out.
Like you, we will not be around forever.
Dance us to pieces and be glad.

Raphael's Goblet

The parcel was large,
the size of a cage.
Had I ordered anything?
The noisy brown paper that wrapped it
like daffodil bulbs

gave way to tissue, white as rice,
gave way to pink
as if I were invited
to inhabit a rose.

At first touch I saw nothing.
Touch whispered: *Try here.*
A goblet so transparent
I nearly missed the stem rising
from a glass nimbus
like a ray of sunlight
as if light had bones,
steady, but tender,
holding its light burden,

this tall, thin-lipped cup
as milky in the making
as if it held fog, or a veil
of smoke from its days
and nights in the fire,

a finger bone from a star.

The Mirror

Who is the fairest one of all?

Flowers without fragrance.
Food a feast for the eye only.
And silence as deep as a stopped heart.
Spiritus mundus.

You let every thing go
forever. All the years we looked
at you and asked your approval,
we lived in your luminous shadow.

Like a good teacher, you showed us
our faults without judgment.
Ah, magic corrupted your purity.
You broke silence, spoke our language.

You see what came of it.

Walking with Glass

Do the six men carry nothing? No.
They carry a sheet of twilight,
tinted glass for the First National Bank.

Three and three,
the great glass between them.
Their palms meet but do not touch.

They do not know they are dancing
in the old way, bearing the weight of silence.
They do not know which man broke stride

and carried the others with him
when the clear body they bore fell
and loosed itself on the men like hail,

as if they who served silence
served it badly.
As if it answered them.

Flying Carpet

Oh carpet, you tuck our dirt away,
hoarding it, hiding it.
Our feet whisper, *Know your place.*
Sweep it under the rug,

hauled out, hung on the line,
the bad beaten out of you,
right down to the warp
where goodness shines through

in threads of silence—
a Persian garden, a paradise
for serpents and butterflies,
on whose sleep we walk.

Scrolled up, you stand in the corner.
Who can translate your alphabet of flowers?
Who can own you without your permission?
Who can ride on the wrist of the wind?
Unroll me like the bud of a lily.
Without wings, without sinews, I am thin as a passport.
Though I do not know the place, I will steer by the stars.
I am the ferryboat of heaven.
Though all seems lost
I will carry you to the one you love.

Legend of the Tangerine

Never hurry a tangerine.

It is too well bred for impatience.
A hassock, stuffed with spices,
seamless as air, offers your tongue
its leathery armor.

Peel without haste; you will come
to a better place.
You are too young to remember

the first tangerine, the festival
of the orange moon, and the night
hung with broad lamps—yes, tangerines
like crystal pumpkins smoky with frost,

and how the priests in saffron prayed
to a moon brighter than blood,
and women knitting themselves in a circle
swelling, then falling away,
quarter by quarter,
As the custom died, the tangerine shrank.
Now it will not even light a closet.

Yet in its sections, you may taste
the women who danced them,
the syllables of their tambourines,

and their lamps blowing—

At the Foundry

Here is an angel, here is a tiger
guarding a nude woman dreaming herself
into marble. Here is a bronze wrestler so big
a visitor fainted; hence the removable fig leaf.
I could lose myself in this foundry.
I am the smallest creature in it.

Things come and go, as God invents them.
May the molten bronze cool.
May the copper rose remember its thorns.
May the pewter bird discover its wings.
May the brass book lie open, indifferent to time,
turning and turning its pages of light.

Still Life with Walt Whitman

For Lewis Hyde

Paint him in his room, eating
his supper from a sheet of brown paper.
Let a tin cup stand there.
Let a bowl stand in front of the cup.
Let a spoon pause on the rim of the bowl,
like a dancer resting.
Let it make peace with the jackknife.
Let the teakettle pipe and hiss
and a fire burn low in the sheet-iron stove.
Let the chairs draw near to listen.
Let the bed warm itself.
Let the pine box cupboard remember its maker,
and when the dishes stand empty,
let him throw the paper into the fire.

Visitation from the Eakins Press

In Memoriam Leslie Katz

No, I can't recall his arrival,
only himself in a dark blue suit,
sitting on the sad sofa
we found in the street.
He held out the pamphlet he'd brought for me:
Author's Rights.

He spoke of his Press, of Jefferson's Bible,
of Whitman. He spoke of American voices
he would publish, printed on the best paper.
He could offer a modest payment.
He wanted to make a book of my stories.
How on earth had he found them?
I would have given them to him for nothing.

III

The Path Not Taken

I took the path into the woods.
The fog unfolded itself, the path sank
into hummocks of moss. Foamflowers
winked their white stars underfoot.
Trees still wearing their lichens
like loosely knit shawls died and fell
silently into the arms of their comrades.
From deep in the woods I heard
the rising arguments of waves, the thwack
and whump of them, slamming the cliffs,
a blow to knock out your breath forever.

At the cliff's edge, a gull flashed the blade
of its wings and caught the current out.
The sea threw up its hands and clattered
into the gorge, shining. I shivered.
What did I know about living in the world?
I carried nothing but the soft-shelled body
I was born with. On the sand lay
charred roots, kelp in rubbery heaps
like abandoned udders, and black rocks
pocked and beaten and rolling like dice.
Stranger, if you sailed a ship you would turn

at the clink of the buoys, chained to the water,
singing of cliffs hidden in the fog's fist.
You would listen for its horn, for its path
as you feel your way through dark waters.

Losing Compass

How well our weather becomes the trees.
Stunned or hooped or lamed by the wind,
their bodies bend to it and hold the pose.
This one, its arm raised,

conducts the tall grass choir it shades
and blesses us. Thatched with reindeer moss
and starflowers, the roots of pitch pines
muscle into the light.

Nothing screeches or whistles or barks. Out of our sight
the wild turkeys camp on the lowest branches.
The deer fold themselves into a sheltered
clearing and sleep all night

on cones and needles. For all things, light
opens the dark woods, the mapped path, the crack
under the door. But who on earth knows where we are?
And which of us remembers the way back?

Bird Land

What is it to be that crow
cruising the ragged oaks,
her crisp feathers not brushing
or breaking the boughs she loves,

or the chickadee, his beak
bearded with cottonwood,
tumbling and springing
to his own tune,

or the hawk as she circles
and drops herself
into the pleats and folds
of the air that obeys her,

or the gull, little rower,
his wings pumping,
stroke by stroke,
crossing the dark water?

Tree House

Start with a tree,
an old willow with its feet in the water,
and one low branch to let you in
and a higher branch to let you
upstairs,
and a lookout branch to show
how far you've come
(the lake before you,
the woods at your back),

and now you are close
to those who live in these rooms
without walls, without doors:
one nuthatch typing its way up the bark,
two mourning doves calling the sun out of darkness,
three blackbirds folding their wings tipped with sunset,
twelve crows threading the air and stitching
a cape that whirls them away
through the empty sky,

and don't forget the blue heron
stalking the shallows for bluegills,
and don't forget the otter backpaddling past you,
and the turtles perched on the log like shoes
lined up each night in a large family,

and don't forget the owl
who has watched over you
since you were born.

Be the housekeeper of trees,
who have nothing to keep
except silence.

Deer in Winter

Four deer make a compass of themselves,
guardians of sleepers under the snow.

Astronomers of the earth, they sniff its constellations
of slugs, moss, acorns, the darkened fingers

of oak leaves. Now they are hungry.
They nose the old grass in the winter garden.

They are all ears for weather and hunters
and their ears are filling their pockets with news.

The February Bee

The bumblebee crept out on the stone steps.
No roses. Nothing to gather.
Nothing but itself, the cold air,
and the spring light.
It rubbed its legs together
as if it wished to start a fire
and wear its warmth.
Under its smart yellow bands
the black body shone like patent leather.
It groomed itself, like a pilot
ready for takeoff and yet not ready:
when my shadow fell over him
he flicked his wings, checking them,
and took off into the bare garden.

The Vanity of the Dragonfly

The dragonfly at rest on the doorbell—
too weak to ring and glad of it,
but well mannered and cautious,
thinking it best to observe us quietly
before flying in, and who knows if he will find
the way out? Cautious of traps, this one.
A winged cross, plain, the body straight
as a thermometer, the old glass kind
that could kill us with mercury if our teeth
did not respect its brittle body. Slim as an eel
but a solitary glider, a pilot without bombs
or weapons, and wings clear and small as a wish
to see over our heads, to see the whole picture.
And when our gaze grazes over it and moves on,
the dragonfly changes its clothes,
sheds its old skin, shriveled like laundry,
and steps forth, polished black, with two
circles buttoned like epaulettes taking the last space
at the edge of its eyes.

Horseshoe Crab

The box pulsed with promises:
Build your own
3-D model of the creature
that crawled out of the past!

What road did your claws follow,
furrowing the sea floor
pulling yourself along?

Carefully separate the model
from the rest of the document
by removing the two staples

from the primal ooze, from sandstone
folding into freedom, from a family
of helmets without war.

Cut out each part along the solid green lines.
Make a mountain fold along the green lines.
Make a valley fold on the white lines.

Notice the loose tongue of the kelp,
black and crisp in the sun.
Notice the heart pumping its coveted blue blood,

without passengers, without ambition,
dreaming itself to deep water.

A Red-tailed Hawk at Home in the World

Nothing turned her gaze away
from the meal she was making,
one foot pinning the dead squirrel
to the tamped earth and treading it,

the other tugging at sinews
like a robin pulling worms after rain,
or my hand correcting an ill-stitched seam,
untying the red strings and slipping

the meat off in splinters close
to the bone, the squirrel's pelt flayed
and unzipped from the flesh,
the head snipped from the stump,

the soft white fur of its underside
still protecting the small hole of its sex,
the killer's cheek pale green, a blush
edging the beak where bits of the meal

hang on her head pumping up and down—
and what a head! The top glazed bright as burned
sugar, the white feathers under it soft as cream,
the sweep of her back stenciled

with whitecaps covering the dark
appetites of the sea, right down to her talons

sharpened like moons, and all this
four feet from the curb and the hum of cars

on their human business.

The Disguise

I pulled the curtain in the dim
stall and turned the silver dial
to hot, and a black wing that cast
no shadow floated from the white
tile to the damp floor. Folded and
shuttered, like a velvet bag
stitched to snuff out light:
give up no secrets.

I have shared falling water
with spiders and geckos
and with my beloved
and the baby we made
but never with this small
undertaker who shares my taste
for clothes in dark closets.
Canyons of steam unwound

around us. It struggled
up the slippery wall, tidy
in its tux, and pious
and dignified in its habit.
Hiding its good side, it took flight
and like a lunar eclipse
turned itself out
of sight.

IV

The Sea at Truro

At low tide, when Water opened
her workshop, her shining hands unrolled
a fabric so light I saw straight down
to the loom on which it was born—

long ropes of sand ridged like muscles
on the sea's floor, seeded with
ghostly pebbles polished like eggs
waiting in weedy nests

and a crab claw hugging its shadow,
and the pleated rim of a clam.
Till the sea threw out a net
that spun itself from the breath of the waves,

in threads so fine I saw its shine
in leaf and stone and the sunset's plumage
and the light that was always there
waiting for me to find it.

The Water Seamstress

The bride admires the pleats on the skin
of the sea. So smooth! So cool!
She fingers the waves, some quilted,
some smocked and gathered

like the dress her mother made for herself
to wear at the wedding, and for the pleasure
of making it and for the company of the light
at play on the satin as it poured through her hands,

and for the white frills on the sleeve of each wave
as it sped along the shore, knitting itself,
row after row, then exploding with joy
and unraveling everything.

The Wave Has No Hands

The wave has no hands.
With its polished crest
it pushes its harvest of stones,
rolls them, pulls them back.

The stones shimmer, they wear
the light of the sun rising.
The tide delivers them,
packed for the journey.

On land, how still they are!
Brides waiting to be chosen,
gifts tied with black ribbons of seaweed.
The sea offers its genealogy of waves,

to the dry sand and moves on.
I hear the stones, their questions,
their patient silence. *What place is this?*
Who will carry us to the next station?

Honor the Waves

Honor the waves as they wash toward you,
wearing the cool skins they are born with,
riding the dark like a congress of nuns.

You can hear the froth of their gossip,
their laughter exploding. Now they show you
their parcels of darkness huddled in husks of light.

A gull hanging on the horizon peers close and deep.
Who's down there? The shadows of trees not born?
Buttons of moonlight on the rim of sleep?

That's when the Sea of Forgottens opens your eyes.
Nothing is closed to you,
not your first journey, not the gleam that lit it,

not the hands that set you down in this world.
Do you remember the day you were born?
Pay attention. I will give you the whole story.

The Live Sea Scrolls

When the Live Sea Scrolls arrive for translation,
roll after roll, as the sea delivers them

wrapped in dark waves for their long journey,
can you hear them? Can you read them?

Have you studied the syntax of clouds?
Can you recite the proverbs of the pearls?

Has the tide taught you its restless alphabet?
Can you follow the path carved by bare feet

fleeing, leaving no other trace of their lives?
When the tide swabs the sand clean

can you speak for those lost in translation?
With your own breath, can you keep them alive?

No Wonder

The sea reads slowly, as old men in libraries
follow the news, forefingers checking off

each word. Where gulls walk the wet sand
the sea erases so many sentences with a sweep

of its paw. I saw the Chinese character
for "man" in the birdfoot language

while the sea rolled up its scrolls,
millions of them. All those letters loose!

No wonder the sea babbles and roars.
No wonder men drown in their own stories.

V

Elementals

Put on my cap of air.
The sun will leap for you,
the moon clatter her hands,
the light swarm into shapes
                    at your commands.

Put on my shoes of fire.
The hills will carry you,
the stones waken and flower,
your hands level and purge
                    mountain and tower.

Put on my garment of water.
The whale shall be your bed,
sunfish your morning star,
seaweeds your lovers crying,
                    we are, we are.

Put on my apron of earth,
the cloth of rain. All things
fall through the net of birth,
                    again again,
put on the earth.

Song for Two Voices

For Ted Kooser

The devil smiled. "How well I know
in the beginning was the fall,
cyclones, floods, the ice and snow,
flesh and whiskers, blood and bones,
the shining eyes of precious stones,
the poison rivers, dirty streams,
the frozen hearts, the dreadful dreams.
From death to death, from birth to birth
I own it all.
In the beginning was the fall."

The poet smiled and shook his head.
"This is a valentine for Earth.
I honor her with words," he said.
"From death to death, from birth to birth,
this restless planet is my home.
In the beginning was the poem."

Ian's Angels

The angels have little tails. Inside them are gifts.
We don't know what their gifts are.

—Ian FitzPatrick, age 5

The first angel Ian drew
was silent as the sun
on empty fields of snow.
Nothing was fast or slow,
the world not yet begun.

The second angel Ian drew
sang green out of the ground.
Birds of the air, rejoice.
Let fire find its voice,
each river its own sound.

The third angel Ian drew
wore vestments pale as sand.
A message printed there
would let earth speak to air.
But from whose hand?

The fourth angel Ian drew
packed darkness in its wings
for planets, bright or dim,
for moons riding the rim
of day. For unborn things.

The fifth angel Ian drew
turned into a door.
It opened into space.
I never saw its face,
only the light it wore.

The Dream Speaks

I am not under the table tented with blankets,
or under the attic stairs,
or in the cellar where jars of tomatoes and pears
sleep pickled in shadows, like leaves bruised
black by six months of snow. Don't look
in the clubhouse shanty lodged in the maple tree,

from which you see
your future: men mowing, women digging out
dandelions—little space pilgrims
globed in light. I am not the oak
from which the soldier spoke

to three dogs guarding the chests of copper,
silver, gold, and the tinderbox in the story.
I live in nobody's story,
not even the mirror's comfortable rooms
booklined like yours, but only the mirror reads
its own writing. Apparition? Dream?
I live in the seam
of sleep and waking and leave my footprints
on time. What did you hope to keep?
In me nothing of childhood is lost,
not even our holy game of hide and seek.

Shedding the Human

I

At night my lady calls the goats,
The white goats grazing the blue pasture.

When I walk by, she hands me her coat.
"Do not refuse me. This is what I do."

When I take it, she follows her sisters.
Nothing can hold her, nothing can hold her.

She was my lady of the blue pasture.
She is my white goat on the holy mountain.

II

First the names went.
Then the nouns, taking their baggage
of fragrance and colors.
Then the structure they lived in.
Their tracks, wiped clean, vanished like snow.
The stations like honeycombs stood empty
till they too disappeared.
The white room? Empty. Silenced.

And far off, the bear began dancing.

Advice to a Traveler

The buffalo suns himself on the black rock.
He is so small he wants to marry my thumb.

—J. P. Chapin, *Celestial Ponds of Tibet*

By the Gate of Fishes the snake is sleeping.
The one you're afraid of.
The one with a thousand scales.
In his scales the moon is rising,
a thousand moons and each one dreaming of you.

Grave

Last year four men planted you under a stone.
Today I plant the dumpy heart of a narcissus.

Sharing your bed, it will wake up singing.

Acknowledgments

With gratitude to my editor, Ann Close, for her good counsel and patience, and to Jean Naggar, for her friendship and support over many years.

Grateful acknowledgment is made to the editors of the following periodicals, where the poems in this book first appeared:

"Calling the Characters," *Pen America*, No. 11, 2009.

"Ian's Angels," *Image*, Fall 2009.

"Shedding the Human" and "Advice to a Traveler," *Caliban*, No. 3, April 2011.

"The Monastery Kitchen," *Field*, Fall 2009.

"At Low Tide," *Spirituality and Health*, July–August 2011. Commentary by Kathleen Norris.

"Bridget's Confession" (original title: "Hindsight"), *The New Yorker*, November 1996.

"The Famous Poet" and "Learning by Heart," *The Hampden-Sydney Poetry Review*, Winter 2011.

"Auction Block," *Open City*, Spring/Summer 2007.

"The Dream Speaks," *Secret Spaces of Childhood*, edited by Elizabeth Goodenough, University of Michigan, 2003.

"An Angel Considers the Naming of Meat," *Field*, Spring 1996.

"Tree House," *A Place for Play*, edited by Elizabeth Goodenough, a companion volume to the Michigan Television film *Where Do The Children Play?* 2008.

"Still Life with Walt Whitman" and "A Red-tailed Hawk at Home in the World," *ABZ: A Poetry Magazine*, No. 3, 2010.

"Unfinished Still Life" (published under a different title), *Shenandoah* 61, No. 2, February 2012.

"The Path Not Taken," *Field*, No. 86, Spring 2012.

A NOTE ABOUT THE AUTHOR

Nancy Willard was educated at the University of Michigan and Stanford University. She has written two novels, seven books of stories and essays, and eleven books of poetry. A winner of the Devins Memorial Award, she has had NEA grants in both fiction and poetry. Her book *Water Walker* was nominated for the National Book Critics Circle Award. She won the Newbery Medal for *A Visit to William Blake's Inn*. She teaches in the English department at Vassar College.

A NOTE ON THE TYPE

The text of this book was set in a typeface called Bell. The original punches for this face were cut in 1788 by the engraver Richard Austin for the typefoundry of John Bell (1745–1831), the most outstanding typographer of his day. They are the earliest English "modern" type design, and show the influence of French copperplate engraving and the work of the Fournier and Didot families. However, the Bell face has a distinct identity of its own, and might also be classified as a delicate and refined rendering of Scotch Roman.

Composed by North Market Street Graphics, Lancaster, Pennsylvania

Printed and bound by Thomson-Shore, Dexter, Michigan

Book design by Robert C. Olsson